T0328753

Published in 2023 by Hands-On Books, an imprint of
Modjaji Books, Cape Town, South Africa
www.modjajibooks.co.za

ISBN 978-1-991240-08-8 (print)
ISBN 978-1-991240-09-5 (ebook)

Editor: Kobus Moolman
Cover design: Marcos Martins
Typesetting: Porat Jacobson

Cover photo: Michael Wessels

ALONE IN THE HOUSE

ALONE IN THE HOUSE

Poems

Michael Wessels
(1958 – 2018)

In memoriam
Of our Beloved Michael
For Akira and Tao

Contents

PREFACE
by Linzi Rabinowitz

We lived as a family in the home that nestled beneath an ancient mistbelt forest in the Byrne valley, KwaZulu Natal. Michael had spent more than a year building this home high up on the hill which had only footpaths as access. It was a back-breaking labour of love but to this day stands as testimony to his uncompromising commitment to live a life resonant with his ideals. It was a place able to nourish his poetic sensibilities as well as hold the daily rituals of working the land, endless hours of reading and writing and the countless footfalls through the forest with his young children.

I can still see Michael seated on the time-worn floral print chair, next to the small Victorian Dover stove in the corner of our kitchen. Our sons are perched on either arm of the chair. Michael is reading and the boys are enraptured. Reading late into the night and sometimes even before school was Michael's way of sharing his passionate love of literature with his boys which extended later even to reading various prescribed university texts to his preteen boys.

For Michael, reading poetry aloud was essential to best experience the poem. Although he consistently brought his intellectual rigour and analytic mind to his teaching and writing, he unfailingly invited his students, friends and family to experience poetry as a spoken and shared encounter to be felt and sensed.

Michael had a mind that ranged freely across the vast terrains of his intellectual and poetic pursuits. This inner world found its counterpoint in his adventurous spirit which led him on foot across wild and dramatic landscapes - sometimes to places of searing solace and beauty and oftentimes to a favourite cave in the Drakensberg with a backpack of poetry and his little black notebooks.

For a long stretch of time, he photographed intimate images of the varied plant life in his much-loved forest. From these images of delicate flowers, intricate fungi, whorls of tree bark and veined patterns of fallen leaves, he wrote Haiku-like poems and prose which might begin with a leaf and end with its suspension between life and eternity.

When trawling through some of Michael's mails after his death, I came across his correspondence with someone who had recently lost a friend to cancer. His words to her now carry a poignant prescience, "Life, we have to drink in all the beauty and bear all the pain". This body of work is a tracery of beauty and an expression of Michael's essence. It is a legacy bequeathed to us and one which allows glimpses into his vibrant and expansive being.

My hope is that our sons, Akira and Tao, will encounter anew their beloved father through these poems and that you, the reader, will find much to think about and feel as you read through this selection.

I am grateful to Porat Jacobson for his sensitive layout of this book and to Marcos Martins for his beautiful cover design. Thank you Colleen for your excellent guidance.

I owe immense gratitude to Kobus for his magnificent determination to bring Michael's work to a wider audience. Both Kobus and Julia offered Michael deep friendship and collegiality. I thank you both for your contributions to this book which help the reader understand Michael's literary sensibility and complexity.

INTRODUCTION
by Kobus Moolman

> I am exhausted with poking at dead poems
> I am waiting for a poem that will fly
> on the wings of its own weight
> words that will cast off their bandages
> and reveal something uncontactable by prayer

We must begin somewhere. So we begin with words. Michael was a man of words.

Words are the names of things. Michael knew the names of so many things. He knew the names of plants. And of trees. Of birds. He knew the names of mountains. And rivers. And mist-covered forests.

Words are the names of cities and towns and villages. They are the names of ideas. Of 'truths the hand can touch,' to quote Athol Fugard.

But words are also the names of loved ones. And the names for loved ones. And they are the names of friends. Michael's name was beloved by many.

Words can be sung. Or they can be prayed. Words can be written down. Or memorised and told and re-told. Over and over.

Words can be wings with which to ascend. Or they can be stones with which to weight something down.

Michael knew the words for both of these shapes of things. For both of these states.

For Michael was a man of many words.

He wrote all his life. His was a life given over to words. Both words spoken (in conversation, in teaching) and words on the page.

'Sometimes poets die before they are dead'. With these stinging words Michael sets off on his long poem 'Spots of Time'. It is an autobiographical poem. As all Michael's poems are.

A poem about journeying. And encounter. And discovery. As so many of his poems are.

But it is a strange poem too. It is made up of many different things. Things that come across to us in different shapes. And sounds.

One shape is in the familiar lyric. With its ragged lines and its tall, slightly awkward first person gait. But gentle all the time. A shape and a sound that we recognise from many others in this book. Another shape takes on the disguise of a travelogue. It pays attention. It names things. Valhalla. Golgotha. The Skeleton Coast. A third shape is that of a story. It tells. In long loping, lightfooted paragraphs.

All of these shapes we recognise as Michael's. Because he knew the names of many shapes.

But there is a darker shape too that lurks in this poem. Even an unsettling shape. As it lurks within all and behind all of Michael's poems here in this book.

It is the shape and the sound of doubt. And inadequacy. The shape of words that struggle for words. Words that are at a loss for words, as it were.

For although Michael was a man of words, of many, many words, still he wondered whether words could be enough. Particularly whether his words were enough. Whether words, his words, could survive on their own: 'nothing with a name / survives on it own', he acknowledges. For he knew that all words slide out and away from the shapes that they name.

Michael wrote for most of his life. For most of his life he had committed his thoughts onto paper. It was what made him who he was. Quite often this took the shape of a personal diary. A small notebook. Some of which his life partner, Linzi Rabinowitz, graciously shared with me. Pocket-sized for portability often. In pencil, or black or blue pen. There might be drawings in these notebooks, and recipes, prayers, chants, meditations, the notation of classical Indian sitar music even. Most often there would be names and telephone numbers and addresses in the back.

How strange to find one's own name and address there! From many, many lifetimes ago. From some few years after we met.

I met Michael in 1987. He was living at Fox Hill, just outside Pietermaritzburg. I was working as a sub-editor at the local newspaper. Michael was doing his MA at the University of Kwa-Zulu-Natal. It was a time of violent political and social contestation in the townships around the city. And the army had moved in to occupy many of these areas. We met over words. Michael lent me the collected works of St John of the Cross, Basho's *On Love and Poetry* and Pablo Neruda's *Memoirs*. (I had written the titles down in my notebook from that year.) We went frequently to the Eddels Sports Club in Mountain Rise to listen to township jazz. We plucked up the courage (fortified no doubt) to read our poems at the Community Arts Workshop in Durban, organised by the local branch of the Congress of South African Writers.

For, apart from everything else in his notebooks, they were esentially meeting spaces for his words. For his poetry. Fragments. First drafts. Unfinished.

For Michael's was a life given over to words. And to the naming of words.

And by the end of his life, certainly, he had been recognised as a man who spoke and who wrote authoritatively with a particular lexicon of words. Words for a particular way of knowing about things. These were exact, methodical, analytical words. About complex things and ideas. The unwritten literature of the San people, for one. Which he wrote about with profound respect. And the politics of eco-criticism, too. Which he wrote about with passion and with moving conviction. Because of course he knew plants and he knew trees and mountains and rivers. And he understood their beings in themselves. On their own terms. Not ours. As he writes in his poem, 'The Thing about Plants': 'each day the wild flowers drag the world / out from the morgue of history and raise it into the light'.

And so by the end of his life Michael had ended up publishing more than thirty articles, papers and chapters in books. Employing precisely such precise words.

Moreover, he had published an acclaimed study, *Bushman Letters*. While a second, a follow-up monograph, was in draft form upon his death. Unfinished. Waiting to be brought to life.

And he had also written an almost two hundred page travelogue cum-memoir, "Travellers in India and Pakistan", based on a two-year journey that he and Lindy Scholtz undertook in the early 1990s through the length and breadth of those two countries. A manuscript that also waits patiently to be brought to life.

All of these names and places and shapes we recognise as Michael's. Because he knew the names of so many places and shapes.

His was a life given over to words.

And it was for his words printed on the page, between the covers of a book, that he desired to be remembered. As a man of words.

And yet, ultimately, despite the importance of these words for him (and they were extremely important for him) they were not the words of his soul. I make no apology for using this word. That is after all its name.

From early on in his life Michael's soul belonged to other words. Words that were in their essence of a solitary nature. That were private in their origin. Though they might very often turn public later on. Words that took on the shape and the sound of inward things. Though they used outward things to talk about them. Words that did not end with thought – as many of his other useages of words did – but started there, in fact, only to move onward, outward, to the limitations of thought. Words, ultimately, that did not shy from feeling. And from feeling for.

For in his inner being, where it mattered most, Michael was a poet. He had the soul of a poet. And he longed to be recognised as such. Having one poem published in a small literary magazine meant far more to him than academic articles in prominent journals.

'The breath and finer spirit of all knowledge,' is how Wordsworth described poetry. But, of course, few of us believe this anymore. Few of us believe in this awful (full of awe) vision of poetic imagination. This overwhelming drive and energy to a form of solitary concentration that embodies that which is invisible and intangible. '[S]omething that listens, not without fear, for something beyond itself, beyond words,' as Paul Celan expressed it.

And yet, at the same time, Michael was only too keenly aware of overblown claims to a poetic identity he could not own:

> with no poems that could be read at twenty
>   and none at fifty
> other people's words already inscribed
> on a headstone in a stolen country

'Spots of Time' was the only poem Michael ever published in his life. At the age of 59. It was published in *New Coin* journal in 2017, just under a year before his death.

Three further poems were published posthumously. In 2018.

A long poem. And three short poems. And the long poem only in the year before his tragic death. A poet unutterably 'left without poems'.

> when God passed on
> his corpse nourished poems like toadstools
> but these could not survive the lights for
>   more than an instant

For what does it take to be called a poet, Michael asks himself in his poetry. And it is a question that he struggled with profoundly. Amidst the shape of all of his words. Both the ones that struggle for words for the world. And the ones that take delight in the world.

For it is not just a question about naming. As easily as naming soul soul.

More profoundly, what does it take to be a poet, Michael asks himself. By that I think he means, how actually – in what ways, roundabout or straightforward – does a poet set about constructing their world and themselves in words? For in the end, it is all about words.

In the end words are all that a writer ever has.

And words are always at a loss for words.

But it is in this failure of theirs to make themselves understood that they become something more than themselves. Something other.

It is in this so-called failure that words redeem themselves from their names. That in the end they 'reveal something uncontactable by prayer'.

We must end somewhere. Inevitably. So we end with words.

Michael was a man of words.

Words are the names of things. Michael knew the names of so many things.

Michael's name was beloved by many.

> A poet's despair is not just personal; he despairs of the word and that implicates all our hopes. Every time a poet writes a poem he is asking the question, Do words hold good? And the answer has to be yes: it is the contrafactual condition upon which a poet's life depends.
> – *Anne Carson*

Photo: Michael Wessels

If your path through life
were as visible as the larva's trail
through the Cape beech leaf,
what would it look like?

Spots of Time

Sometimes poets die before they are dead

Wordsworth's ghost climbed Helvellyn
with stamps fluttering around the corpses of his children
a crumbling sister and archangel
left in an attic in the village below

still the singing sang on
sings still from the radio in the daffodils on the traffic
   island

Sylvia Plath pushed her head into an oven

some poets stuck their heads in their poems
a few perished inside the prisons
others died waiting outside
one was hunted down and shot hiding in a metaphor

when God passed on
his corpse nourished poems like toadstools
but these could not survive the lights for more than an
   instant

poets were left without poems

not all the poets disappeared when the poems stopped
as would have been appropriate
you can spot a few even now clinging to words like
   pensions
snouting among coffee shops and smart bombs

staring wild-eyed at the colours
in the supermarkets scaring the shoppers
queuing meekly at the tills
clutching packages of meat and memory sticks
a menace also on the roads
knocking into images or falling off unlicensed anapaests

with no poems that could be read at twenty and none at
    fifty
other people's words already inscribed
on a headstone in a stolen country
poetry I discovered too late could not withstand
too much desire for things with no existence
or no desire for them

Rilke's unicorn had galloped back into the tapestry a
    century before
I went searching for it in the hot hills of the Magaliesberg

Ginsberg sat above the railway tracks
with a friend and a sunflower

one morning I stood on the edge of the tarmac
without a friend among the khaki weeds
the sun underlined things a car deletes
rats rummaging in cans and packets
road stones stuck like broken teeth in black toffee

the road to Durban outside Warden on only one winter's
day standing among white hobos with cardboard cases and
hangovers like toothache who took three weeks getting to
the warmth while for a boy with a guitar and a dream it was
only a day

no poetry or bunny chows in the Free State in '79
only the police sticking their fat fingers like penises up
    rectums
looking for dagga and sedition
there was always a bitter story coming closer in a yellow
    van flashing blue lights
on Sundays the sermons of the dominees
spread across the veld
like poison gas from the idiotically beautiful sandstone
    churches

the women too were patriarchs especially the women

we travelled constantly between houses thousands of
kilometres apart set among painted mine dumps or
mango trees where fruit bats sounded or in the mandrax
streets beneath the mountain the houses had painted
corrugated iron walls and wooden verandas on stilts and
were populated permanently by tabby cats and temporarily
by travellers with an orange and the sky in their rucksacks
and there were also the comrades hiding out in the suburbs
vanishing at each creak of the gate reappearing shortly
afterwards breathless but calm growing lean on a diet of
drugs revolution township jazz most significant were the
kisses as the sun rose under the sheets in the cicada high
mornings or so it seems or so it seems now when all that
remains is the ache of memory like an open wound

in a way that drew no inspiration from the sky on the road
or off the road living next to it or travelling on it or rolling
the toy cars in the red dust making the engine noises oneself
it wasn't only tarred roads there were dust roads and paths
and ways where there were no paths and at the beginning

the routes along the branches of the apple tree in the garden
in Parkwood the poetic sensibility was formed exactly in a
break in the glass shards on the brick wall above the alley
where the refuse men came joking in Bhaca and also the
police in the early morning to haul naked husbands from
the arms of the women who fed and bathed us but were
precisely not our mothers as the frost lay on the city and the
Black Marias swallowed the light

it was far from there to piles of hot naan outside bakeries on
frozen mornings and the heads of the Buddhas at Bamiyan
on which we stood years before the Taliban exploded them
but also

not too far and it began with a wooden horse and a red
tricycle under the mulberry boughs moving through the
garden ways that were also the world one morning I pushed
open the coal shed door leaning against it with all of a three
year old's strength all at once it flew open and a coal black cat
leapt at me with claws afire but not before I'd glimpsed the
kittens I'd come to see blood welled as I fled to my mother's
floral print dress I wouldn't know for another twenty years
that it was the time of the treason trial

on winters' nights the policemen came
boots crunching the frost
pretending they could not hear my mother's reproaches
grumbling in Afrikaans and Sotho
shamed by her words and her beauty
looking through the panes distorted by frost I saw
the woman who loved me by day
shivering in petticoats her hair different
they were dragging a man into the van

eyes swam behind the grill like small white fish

we walked through the park in spring
I recall her soft smell half a century later and her laugh
but not her face or a name
it looked like a village green but it wasn't anything
    innocent
as she joined the knots of black women sitting on the grass
beside the empty benches
while I raced the children the dogs the ducks
and every tree blossomed
in the radiant Highveld air

visiting the animals in the zoo with my mother
for purposes of commiseration the hyenas
and wild dogs in the strongest-smelling enclosures
eliciting the most and the shaggy polar bears sagging in
    the heat
after feeding monkey nuts to the elephants I flew
up the terraces on Valhalla's wings towards the war
    memorial
and the avenues of planes and jacarandas
forgetting my mother remembering she was there
as I clambered over the retired steam engine manufactured
    by Krupps in 1938

in the photograph the face of a child in corduroys
and the face of a red and white mongrel
meet in the dog's enamel bowl
pale blue and chipped
it would turn up again in a line of poetry fifty years later

with one of a laughing father spraying the boy with a
    hosepipe

decades before words would catch up to the event
and reveal it as a small family tragedy

still book 1 of *The Prelude*
a children's party in the valley of the thousand hills
nine years old breathless in the chase the beauty of the
    world
pinned me to the ground the excited shouts of boys
displaced by cricket shrill and frogs
I knew then that the mist which moved across the valley
through the sugar cane
moved through me also

sometimes making a poet can be a messy business
especially tacking together a poet without poems
ten years old on a train a pudgy man
pushed me into the toilet awash in misdirected urine
from white penises only
wheezily eager he opened his fly and put my child's hand
onto his man's erection I screamed without knowing why
the metal wheels ground the rails
ground my screams
I bit into the wrist that held me time veering on a gold
    watch before my eyes
I bit and bit and he released me knowing
I'd say nothing to my mother with whom he'd been
    amiably chatting
and would continue chatting until the station at Port
    Shepstone

sitting in the lotus among ericas and restios
where the winds off the Atlantic and the Indian oceans
    cross

my eyes opened into a caracal's eyes a foot away
I cannot tell what the wild cat saw
but I who had been waiting on a vision from another
    world
received a vision from this one

waiting on the road outside East London hour after hour
the sun pitiless as the motorists
the ride when it came stopped two hundred metres away
not for me I thought until I saw the men beckoning and
    ran
only as far as Port Elizabeth they said
but it wasn't Port Elizabeth but New Brighton
a night stop on the road to Cape Town
the gang leader squatted half a metre away
my life trapped in his brain
eyes lit by mandrax twisted mine
like a wet yellow towel
to flinch was death I knew
knives in the hands of the men in the shadows
the trochaic metre of their breath
ancient and current hatreds barbed wire night
women and children in a doorway hushed
time stalled a killing screened on the township night
then the man held up a bottleneck against the moon
I took it sucked on the brown rag until the pipe hissed
a white boy blowing dagga smoke into the black township
    night
the veins in the man's neck stopped pulsing eyes settled
    back in the face
the kitchen sounds and the children's games resumed
the pipe moved from hand to hand

at dawn a group of men bribed with furniture that would never make the crossing from suburb to suburb dismantled a fence to free the truck stuck in the alley and the journey's routines resumed cleaning the stalks and pips from the cheap matchbox dagga crushing the mandrax pills swigs from the brandy bottle through the nights through the burning days hills plains towns turns with the truck stop girls on the finest double mattress in the back abrupt intimacies ripped into the blood vinegary chips and white loaf meals stars pointing at my heart a tarpaulin catching fire outside Beaufort West "Kyk hoe die fokken larney se lorry brand nou," laughed the men sprawled on the tar of the N1 swigging from the brandy bottle two days two nights of sweet sin in a shebeen before the relief truck arrived and the drive to Cape Town was completed and once again it was just the battered rucksack moving along a street in Woodstock among wind-blown packets

I soaked the seeds from the nursery shop until they
    sprouted brains
and drank them ground into strawberry sap
angels stuck little white hooks into my skin
the air broke
I had crawled to a tap in the outhouse off the farm veranda
when turning I saw it
a Mozambique spitting cobra
taller than a man come to kill framed in the door in a
    painting of the sky
I flew through the window
and roamed the hillside through the day and the night
with flashing eyes and floating hair
next day I learned the snake the seeds had conjured up had
spat venom into a friend's eyes and we piled on the back of

a bakkie and drove through the acacia thorn and Victorian
town to the hospital on the hill to fetch him

the memories that cannibalise life are the only ones that
    live on
there were the smooth legs that led to a murder in a
    garden
there was the way she called my name deep in the fleshy
    folds of nights
in a mansion built of blood and betrayal
while rain beat at the hut
there was wind in the forest and screech hyraxes when the
    moon shone
and a house that was reached from above down a
    mountain path
a crooked house in a tale that is still being told
the great hearted man wouldn't cut the trees
so we built the house around them
he sang love songs as he hammered
while I bore the planks we'd cut in pine plantation across
    the valley
past the guitar player under the eaves and the woman I
    dreamed of in the garden
and was compared to Christ on the road to Golgotha

spots of time
paint spattered on canvas

once there were three in a day
carved deep on the silver trophy of the life that death will
    win
the way out of Zanskar followed the scree of the sheer
    ravine the horsemen with a thousand horses told us as

they clattered past in the turbaned light
at dawn we began the ascent
hour after hour climbing
up into the white
the track erased by snow
my lover vanished and I stopped to die there too
then once more the red dot of her jacket moved in the
    silence
and on we fought
upwards through snow deeper than ourselves
scrabbling at the air with the nails of our lungs
until we saw the prayer flags fluttering at the top of the
    pass
like joy
marking the crossing between realms
more than alive we dropped down the other side

at the end of the day we reached green pastures
but there was still a river in flood to cross
melted snow waters thrashed
too wide for the length of rope we carried
I waded then into the second spot of time
death took me before fate
lifted me to the other shore

the third came out of the night and out of our fear
turbaned men knives in teeth squatting silently in the
    starlight coiling a rope
preparations for murder
then they lay down abruptly as children and slept where
    they had sat
said their prayers before dawn broke and vanished

metaphors pasted in the album
memories squeezed out like the juice from bitter berries
and stored in rows in bottles
still I hear the collision of traffic in my mother's throat
and unwrap the paper of life to find pain ticking
like a bomb that is always going to explode
pasting metaphors into the album
idly flipping the pages as Sunday afternoons gurgle down
    the sink hole
packing the lineages into chests of drawers with moth balls

what forms a poet
even one who hasn't written poetry
precisely which words exact their revenge
biding their time as they skulk behind the years
how to weigh books
against conversations in rooms or
bones on the Skeleton Coast

Wordsworth was right
in the end it comes down to rock pools
basking and bathing alternate on a summer's day
in the Magaliesberg
kissing perfect girls
after watching them swim in the cold pools
first their knees then their dark pubic hair and hard
    nipples submerged
radiant teeth and hair as they break the water's surface
splashing the sun
now they sit in beaten chairs tough old women on
    verandas sipping the years from tall glasses
fierce and mysterious as ever
their children gone out into the world

like the poets I too went to school
grey pants grey socks
shoes on feet that had never before worn a shoe
headmaster stalking the corridors
collecting children from the classrooms for beatings in an
    office that reeked of children's fear
moments stuffed with terror
moments overflowing with the overwhelming beauty
of the world as the bell rang and birds flowers children
    poured out of the sun

spots of time
passing through jacaranda leaves
playing on the class room walls
dappling a woman's skin
as she sleeps under a wild plum in the Wolkberg
slanting through the bars of a prison cell in Nelspruit
unravelling in wild coast estuaries
spots of time
glittering in the children's voices

flowers caught in a net of air.

On Reading Coleridge's "Kubla Khan" again

I am exhausted with poking at dead poems
I am waiting for a poem that will fly
on the wings of its own weight
words that will cast off their bandages
and reveal something uncontactable by prayer

finally I glimpse a poem slipping through the garden
a small animal
a mongoose I think with black and yellow fur
it glares at me an instant with eyes like blueberries
and is gone through a gap in the ferns.

On Poetry

A poem doesn't need ink
or a page with words
these are alibis while
the poem happens elsewhere

but a poem does require a victim
installed on a patch of grass near the highway
a victim foolish enough to mistake
theft for a bestowal

a poem should be well-behaved
shun inspiration
just as soon as it doesn't have to
it should end

not like this one that will go on simply
because it can't stop telling its analyst in free verse
about how it thumbed a lift on a shooting star
after it slid out into the world
through a filthy birth canal in a man's head.

Calpurnia Leaves

Botanists managed long ago
but poets are yet to explain
the difference between compound and simple leaves

compound leaves understand light best
they know what to do with raindrops
they are also good with dew

just for an instant
the tree pretends
to be a girl
fanning her face
with Calpurnia leaves
a girl threads the air
around her throat
with a string of green beads.

Crossberry Flower

The sunbirds
have waited all winter
for the crossberry to flower

out of the flower steps
a young man
and a young woman

he boards a bus
carrying a smile like an umbrella
she runs across a grassland in autumn
in a picture pasted on a wall
covered in graffiti

neither knows they have passed the other
or why they stop to admire a crossberry flower
fallen on a wet sidewalk.

Tree Roots

If Michelangelo had been able
to avert his eyes from a heaven
populated by ancient Greeks
not those modern ones smoking cigarettes
at tables near the pier when the ferry comes in
he would have painted the roots
of a giant sour plum tree
with their torsos and tortured forms

now the best we can do
is to finger the roots with our imaginations
it is a thankless task
one only a few rural poets still think necessary

who else has the time to pay attention
to roots let alone dead leaves
scattered ankle deep across the forest floor
things whose souls do not ascend into the sky like flies.

The Thing about Plants

Is that they have a sense of locality
and their newspapers never fail to mention
that air is as tangible as earth

they have integrity
aren't responsible for climate change
don't exploit rape or murder
don't eat meat
don't even eat salad

they might not make the catwalks
but plants are beautiful

plants could be blamed for political passivity
many have allowed themselves to be enslaved on
    plantations
others have been turned into the pages of right-wing
    newspapers
some have let their leaves be eaten by politicians

the truth is though that plants have held out for millions
    of years
and are not about to surrender
weeds push through paving stones
trees stand unyielding on the sidewalks
lilies shine through the smog

and each day the wild flowers drag the world
out from the morgue of history and raise it into the light.

Spinnekopblom

Walking on sand as fine as sea salt
I have passed them each day for a month now
each time they grab me like a hand
as I move through the fynbos rehearsing answers to emails
they stick eyes on my face and inject time into my veins
their colour is not yellow not brown
apricot the books say but apricots are never this colour
unless they grow away from the sun like mushrooms

I looked for them in the book leafed through it again and
    again
and one afternoon I found them hidden
in a small photograph against a background of pink
    watsonia
wachendorfia paniculata it said or Spinnekopblom
no English common name
nothing left of their other names no Khoi or San
no Xhosa either even though the distribution map extends
    to the eastern Cape
spinnekop
spider head flowers
and there is something spidery about the way they hang in
    the air
something also of the texture of silk in their flowers

I walk every day along the mountain path above the
    suburb
a wild place that has nothing to do with the bills the
    marriage
the trailer the unread books arrayed on the shelves

nothing to do with the drive to work through townships
    and shanty towns
the university and its upheavals the emails the newspapers
it is taboo to say that a flower is more important than
    people
more important than the poor
but let me just say that spinnekop flowers
dress better than people that much Jesus got right

I read now in the book that they grow only after fire
two seasons after the arsonists
have set the mountains alight and the helicopters carrying
    pouches of water
have fought the flames
and there is nothing to see on the mountain but ash and
    sand.

A Buddleja Leaf on a Forest Floor

Just
a dead buddleja leaf
is God still counting

a fish with scales
a cartoon kiss
a boat (to the other world)

a slug would look like this if
slugs were beautiful

a dead leaf

it has a mathematics
an unrepeatable colour scheme
it is radically political
an indigenous leaf
a remnant of African forest in the midlands of KwaZulu-
    Natal
in a propertied world of plantations and cows and labour

but is it actually a leaf
or an artefact
swallowed by a camera
excreted by art?

The Esplanade at Durban

The burnished girls
clean their fingers
with long wet tongues outside the chicken outlet
reminding him of browsing impala

the gulls on the boardwalk
make her think of bus conductors
until their elemental cries
drag the city under the waves

ships hover
on the horizon
peddling dreams
no-one
any longer
knows how to dream.

A Park in Durban

From a bench they watched
a sunbird stab the flowers

heard far away
the voices of the pigeons
wrapped
in duffel coats

thus the days were discarded
along with the paper cups.

Sitting at a Window Durban Evening

Cat
slinks among
the tropical undergrowth

a smell in the wind
like bleeding meat
something unknown carried ashore
on a tide of light

surge of sea against the city
flesh falling on concrete

somewhere in the world
in another place altogether
a man bends into a cold wind.

Beach at St Michaels-on-Sea

Children tentatively
finger the desireless labia
of anemones

still the sea pools hold out
on behalf of something
extraordinary

fishermen cast the water
for the images
which will always elude them

at some point the question
of the redemption of angels
will arise

aeon after aeon
the sea hurls itself at the rocks
or so it seems
to a young woman reading
Mrs Dalloway on a bench

on the bed of the sea
blind fish and sea serpents
slowly copulate
or thread their eggs
on strings of brine.

South Coast Summer

Children's laughter
or is it the wind
rattling the banana palms

passion's acolytes
have all disappeared
down the paths through the sugar cane

holidaymakers
still search for excitement after midnight
revved engines
signalling failure or success

the voices in the room have gone now
leaving puddles on the carpets
tooth marks in the walls

nothing wth a name
survives on its own.

A Night down the South Coast

Slate
blank
but for the hand which
has erased the images
from its surface

solemn hymn of gears and engine rush

stung taste
her creases
her sea-tossed hair

vagrant pilgrims
decked in chains
almost free

tinsel and urine-coloured
the drunken voices
scrape crookedly
against the moon.

Beach at Mtunzini

The line between
ocean and sky
dissolved

sandpiper prints
too overlain to be intelligible

a tree frog in the dune forest
tests its notes
falls silent

a man watches a woman
he does not know
stooping on brown legs
to fill a basket
with seashells and bits of driftwood

he runs the sand
through his fingers
surprised by its coloured grains

she straightens
basket in hand
framed by foam and waves

the wild fig leaves in the dunes
burn with red tips.

At Lake Sibaya

The sun
is a toad
luridly
squatting
in an etching of an acacia

her hair
smells like a fresh wound
as she comes out of the water

high above
an eagle tears the blue fabric

far below
a man trudges through a narrative
of his own telling
and does not look up.

Kalahari Mid-day

Lizards lie charging
on the stones

a starched sheet
on a sick-bed
the light stretched out

the movements of the gemsbok
choreographed by that mad artist
the sun.

Ndedema Shelter

As day fell
an eland
fled across the cave wall
it was then that she ordered
a poem
of clay and wild birds' eggs.

They Speak
(After //Kabbo)

They speak they move they make their bodies move
filing out of the pages of the South African history book
like ghosts in the sunlight

they speak they move they make their bodies move
they order the others to be silent
the trees should not speak
the quagga's mouths are stopped
only the stones call out
pleading with the shoppers to buy them.

Walking in Crete

We stopped
in an old town

heard the language
of its stones

crickets split
the night's sticks

at dawn
the sun poured through
a gash in the dark
and set the shoes waiting
at the door alight.

Bullock Cart – Madhya Pradesh

Shrill mid-day sun
no tree or bush
to bring relief
to eye or mind

rutted track
an emaciated man
on a laden bullock cart
ten metres behind
a woman haunts the dust
sari hanging from her bones
like a sloughed snake skin

a load
on her head
always a load

the bullock stumbles
falls on its knees in the stones

wearily she hands
the load from head to earth
hacks at the animal's flank
with a claw of a foot
the great creature labours to its feet
foaming at the mouth

a vision of a drunk crawling up stairs
arrives from another world.

Amber Fort – Rajastan

Walls cross the naked hills
like seams on a thigh

once a stage for heroes and horses
now only dust moves
in the over-heated wind

high overhead
vultures scan the land
for signs of life receding

faltering animals
pocked with shattered mirrors
women
broken by labour and beauty

here in the fort
tourists dutifully wander
guidebooks in hand
cameras ready to shoot
at the first hint
of an image trying to escape

the eyes of the idol
in the shrine
see more than they do

boys fly paper kites
from the ramparts

sun blazes on all.

Stopping for the Night on a Journey on Foot

A wayside inn
looms in the mist
like a lantern lit from within

there are other invitations to answer though
a bed of leaves in the woods
a pillow of roots
the welcome of stones
cold streams
the hospitality of thorn bushes.

Sleeping out in Baltistan

Awakening in a field
he sees
grass beaded with dew
blue-bells with black and yellow centres
purple hyacinths
sheaves of wheat
drying on a stone wall

a robin on a boulder
fragile as porcelain

not he thinks
at all like the bitter-tasting
banana-beaked
foul-mouthed
cheaply painted birds
of the home
he cannot remember.

Zurich Airport in Transit

The people in transit adrift
like readerless poems caught in the headlights
the old the young cruelly thrust together leading suitcases
instead of dogs I wonder if I might get coffee without
    Swiss currency
and what am I doing here flying deeper into the northern
    winter
but it doesn't feel like flying

outside through the rain running down the glass walls
Switzerland
wooded autumnal hills a few steep roofs
I visited 40 years ago
now I could as easily walk on the moon
I have no visa am not fleeing persecution
all I can do is see if it is possible in an airport in transit
to write a poem and derive consolation from it.

Munich Airport

Only robust similes thrive
metaphors wither unseen
metonymy rings the security alarms

black chairs in rows like hooded monks
Lufthansa aircraft waiting outside like
sharks without teeth
people holding phones as children cupping birds do
people sitting as though waiting for bad news in a hospital

sometimes even similes fail
people pulling suitcases on wheels
do not seem comparable to anything
except perhaps an ox yoked to a wheelbarrow
and the ceiling reflected on the floor
and the floor reflected on the ceiling
only resemble each other.

Lost in the Forest

Only for the caracal
is this the way home
past orange toadstools
rooted in night.

Morning Rain

Children's voices
drift up the valley
along with mist
and doves

sagewood flowers bright
in the grey morning

as usual
a flock of forest weavers
peck among the clover

then the mist
turns to rain
so fine
it sounds warm.

The Utility of Words

Bats singing
unheard in the night

the ripped-red hour
strung
like flesh on a wire

nothing to rely on
but ordinary words
lantern cabbage
cardboard ice.

Reflections of an Insomniac

Awakened again
by angels wrestling in the mud
grunting
in their high-pitched register
like mice
being killed

history is a bunch of deities
indifferently gazing
at nothing
not a doting grandparent

the days are too old
for their contents
gaudily rattling
in the nets.

Morning Tea

Between each sip of tea
the morning reveals itself
as a net of luridly coloured
bird calls.

View from the Veranda

White peaks
burnt hills
nothing
in between

birds know more
about living

single cloud in the sky
moving.

Alibi

The church bells that woke me this morning were not
    church bells
only my i-phone simulating the sound of bells
that don't ring in China
but singing in the bushes outside were birds
not recordings of foxes squealing

when I walked past the dining room to the kettle in the
    kitchen
no ghosts were seated at the table and outside the window
on the washing line were hanging clothes not condemned
    men

I brushed my teeth not my soul
then drove off to work and never went to the den
on the banks of the Thames to buy opium or thought
    about
Fellini's La Dolce Vita even once on the drive between
    Kalk Bay and Bellville.

Reflections on the Rubbish

*Italo Calvino's contribution to the household's domestic routines
was to take out the rubbish. Digging in the bin one day, he found
an essay about the individual and the city.*

The truck comes before dawn on a Monday for the black
    bags
later another truck arrives to take away the clear bags
    containing the recyclables
two bags one transparent and virtuous displayed in the
    open
the other hidden in a black bin as shameful as a secret

into the black bag goes everything that cannot be
    redeemed
melted down, resurrected
rotting broken mangled things
a handful of teeth or a severed hand
syringes condoms vomit-soaked rags
coffee grounds and broken glass
the black bags are knotted tossed into the bin
wheeled out onto the pavement when no-one is looking

the reeking garbage truck comes before dawn
manned by men who cackle and leap and crash
like hags in a Disney cartoon
stirring the neighbourhood dogs to a frenzy

the recyclables go into a transparent bag
here everything is recuperated
declared put out in the light of day
whisky bottles and fresh juice bottles made one

porn magazines redeemed along with religious pamphlets
collected by quiet men in a clean truck
gliding smoothly up the road in the afternoon
leaving the dogs to slumber undisturbed.

Newlyweds

A crab drags
a woman through the window
a man kicks its testicles
she spits in its mouth
it scuttles off
an unrepentant look in its eye
she removes the squids
from her eyelids

he pickles a pear
in the micro-wave
these little assurances
are required
he knows from the self-help book
on the shelf of the holiday home
on honeymoons
at the sea-side.

Untitled

His desire was to drown
in sea-dark hair

later he would announce
to men on a bridge
that faith was betrayal

an untitled poem
bobbed in the water below
an object without a word

a vagabond studies
the caprice of boots
their noises
their distances
the cobbler measures
only the fit of a shoe
the pain in the fingers

spirit
a tic in the brain
a wind on the path
the sensation of living
we attribute to the fleshed

yes the woman would have said
as she climbed the steps
on mauve shoes
flesh is clay
and the soul disappears into light
like breath into a shattered balloon

spirit is a pendulum strapped
to a heartbeat.

Desire

I do not know who you are
it is your absence
I celebrate and mourn

I dreamed I held you in the heather
we danced on the flowers

you never lived
and now you have died

the words of love were velvet butterflies
that never found the light

never again will your eyes flash
as you leap into a cold rock pool
nor crows
feast on your livid gems.

Alone in the House

He studies his paint-stained hands
the nails rimed with earth

at night the silence is filled
with insect shrill
the yelp of dogs
from cold yards down the valley

a woman's things
in boxes in the shadows
books dresses driftwood

her words
spoken years ago
stuck in the cracks
of the floorboards.

Evening in the House on the Hill

Confident of its enterprise
an ant crosses the mat
on which I sit recalling

how the sun struck all day
gouging out the crabs' flesh
until only a cemetery
of clawed shells
remained on the beach

and also how years ago
we stopped to eat wild raspberries
as we crossed the Pyrenees
into France on an autumn morning

this morning
the black and khaki hills
lie implacable

the first rains fell days ago
but no-one could guess
that roots and shoots
are stirring within the charred soil

later there is an adder on the path
speaking in tongues
flaunting its evil beauty

thirty years ago
I drove all day to you
trying to keep the wild flowers

on the seat beside me from wilting

in the decades that followed
the sounds of your living beside me
became part of the days along with the sun and the rain

night absorbed now
in its own fat flesh
a butterfly
would be a transgression

the flufftails keen
in some unintelligible
depth of the forest

I cannot hear the wood owls
but they are out there also
flitting in the wind
squatting on darkened branches

sitting here
old bones
in a skin bag
the siren songs singing still
in the blood
like the life left spinning
in a beheaded chicken

the boots in which we walked
tramping tramping still
through the mountains of Pakistan
without us.

Dead at 42

The snow
has forced
the dead tree to bear flowers
just the tip of a cottage roof
not yet white

out of her mouth
no words no breath
only snow

bones of flowers
press down
on the dark

long ago
arms lifted
as the black silk dropped
she turned a woman
seen only by the blind sockets
of the old lemonwoods

at dawn
in a fracture in the rock
we discovered
the refuse of eternity
cat fur snake scale
ghost of samango monkey

now in the dry days
when on cliff edges
Aloe and Natal bottlebrush

break out in blood flowers
she follows the bees down
the scarlet throat of the Greyia blossom

the purple senecios
have gone before spring
blown away as seed in the wind
nor does she wait for the rains
or even the blue fire flowers
the weight of the sky
crushes her
the sunbirds
will not stop singing

while all eyes are on the plants
sending shoots
through burnt grassland
in the forest a rock flowers
her hands
reach out through the stone
to hold up the torch lilies

I see her still
kneeling to breathe in
the perfume of the satyrium
we dance again
on the grass
that grows out of the ashes

by moonlight from shades of night
the felicia mixes its colours

the call of a black cuckoo sounds
too short the season of the harebells

caught in a spider's web
only raindrops
and a single white petal

once I dropped armfuls of wild wet lilies
into her lap
the birds were new then
the stone steps
rain-rinsed web-strung

now the world her flesh
insubstantial
as mist

it would be just another
morning
were it not for the calpurnia flowers

and the scent of the carissa
white
as its flowers.

The Secret Garden

You visit this place. Yet its paths remain untouched by your feet. The waters of its fountains never mingle with the sweat of your flesh or cool your throat. Its soil has been made fertile not with the toil of your hands or the blood of your veins, but by the longing in your heart.

Without your knowing it, the fragrance of infinity leads you through the gates of sleep and out along a way strewn with stars to this garden in which God reclines on the sweet grass, the universe flung across Her shoulders like a sequined shawl. You have glimpsed this place with open eyes once or twice perhaps when you stood on the edge of an abyss or saw through a chink in a stone. You cannot recall it now, only the feeling it provoked in your flesh. It could be an oasis, you imagine, a place of birds and splashing water islanded by sand and fire. Perhaps it lies hidden in forest or ocean. Were there marble steps winding down through coral, and fish of many colours? Could it have been the fresh breath of children which makes your skin tremble at a recollection your mind cannot apprehend? Whenever you encounter beauty or goodness, a scented breeze teases your senses but you cannot imagine what it is which has quickened the air. There is no restlessness so deep as that which attends the incipient remembrance of this place. It is only here that you have truly lived. But it has always eluded you.

Let us go there now, you and I. It is very close. Follow me through this gap between the trees. It is the secret garden. Yes, it was the hands of your imagination which sowed the seed and tended the beds, now dry and neglected. These are the flowers of your stirrings. See how resilient they are;

wilted and drought-stricken, yet still clinging to life in the hard earth littered with gems. We will loosen the soil with these tools, fashioned by unknown hands from hardwoods and antelope horn. The earth is as sensual as the flesh of lovers when we crumble the clods in our hands. If we allow our hearts to roam free, a spring will bubble up and fill this pool in the centre of the garden. Let us replenish the roots of the plants with its water. How the flowers dazzle instantly in the play of light – vermilion, molten gold, blue as lapis, white as the sun.

Nor are we alone. There are birds, frogs and butterflies. And here are those we love most but forgot we knew. Children rush from their play in streams and glades to fling lithe arms about us. Men and women in the long summer of beauty bring their lips to ours and hold us in eager arms. Ancient people with light and laughter leaping from their eyes look at us with the regard of God.

Often we had thought we had arrived in the garden. But it was only forms borrowed from there which taunted our senses, cruelly exciting the blood. Soon the fabric began to fray. The waters curdled and the stones sickened. The air became overburdened. Something stabbed at the pits of our bellies. Children shrank from us with abused eyes. Affection elicited contempt. Paradise turned into a suffocating cage from which we fled, choosing anywhere in preference. Although the waters still ran and colours continued to spill from the flowers, it seemed to us as though we were in a desert of ravening lions.

We knew that we had to find the source of the contamination in our own souls. And so we mined deep, for many long, dreary years, trying to reach the gold we struggled to believe lay beneath the sullen layers of meat. And all the while the memory of the garden receded until it existed only feebly and sporadically on the margins of consciousness from where, if it were ever admitted to awareness, it was as a voice mocking us about the illusory nature of that joy which we had once believed to be the tempo of existence. Still we went within, more now from habit than from determination or hope of deliverance. But we couldn't dissolve in the acid of reflexivity. The morose avenues never once opened up to admit a gleam of light or a breath of air. Nothing could penetrate hearts fixed so obstinately on the void. In the outside world we gossiped and worked but this life went no deeper than did the clothes we pulled over our bodies each morning.

One day on a jaunt to the country with friends to whose importunate invitation it was less tiring to accede than to resist, we found ourselves at the foot of a stone stairway which twisted up through galleries of forest. Light smashed instantly through the walls we had erected around our senses. And we mounted the stairs we knew, although we did not know from where.

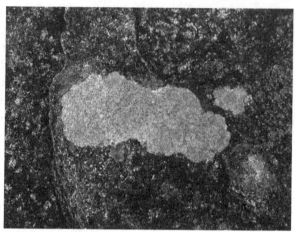

Photo: Michael Wessels

Stray clouds of lichen on the rock:
without its unfathomable mysteries
life would be incomprehensible.

AFTERWORD
by Julia Martin

That Joy

> Let us go there now, you and I. It is very close. Follow
> me through this gap between the trees. It is the secret
> garden.

I'll begin at the end, which is also the beginning. The last piece, a prose poem, returns to a place in the imagination which Michael calls the secret garden. It's a place half-seen, half-remembered, a place we recognise in our hearts, but don't know how to reach anymore. Most of the collection is about... access to this mystery, to another world inside of this one. We may have forgotten where to find the portal, but the poems invite us to discover it again: to see.

The way in is often through the wild. Michael himself loved gardening, but in many of the poems the secret garden is undomesticated. Its wildness is ineradicable, the poems suggest, and the interconnected world of nonhuman beings endlessly inspiring. A mongoose slips through with the freshness of a poem, calpurnia leaves are beaded with dew, a crossberry flower is a transport to a magical place, and the roots of a giant sour plum tree draw the eyes down out of the skies. Here, and again and again, though the speaker might long for transcendence, the vision he receives is in opening all his senses to the living world. As Michael writes after meeting a caracal on the mountain, 'I who had been waiting for a vision from another world / received a vision from this one.' Often this seeing is catalysed by flowers. In 'Dead at 42,' a poem near the end of the collection, the gathering of wild flowers in the memory is at once an act of grief and of renewal: aloes, bottlebrush, greyia blossoms, purple senecios, harebells, lilies, satyriums… I'm reminded of the mound of flowers we all picked from the mistbelt to place on Michael's coffin. As he writes in another poem about the resilient hopefulness of plants, 'and each day the wild flowers drag the world / out from the morgue of history and raise it into the light.'

Inevitably then, the life of the garden is an ongoing conversation with death. Our lives are harsh and fleet and terrifying and confusing, and the imagination of the seer or the poet, the eye of vision, must know death too: death which makes life vivid. So in the extraordinary long poem 'Spots of Time' which describes moments of intense awareness that open a gateway to the mystery of being, the growth of a poet's mind is nurtured by trauma as well as by beauty. The child feels a continuity with 'the mist which moved across the valley' and the same child is abused by a pudgy man in a train toilet. The child grown to a man hitches a scary ride with mandrax gangsters, kisses perfect girls in a Magaliesberg rock pool, and has three near-death experiences in one day on a trek through the mountains of Ladakh. In telling the stories of these experiences as an assemblage of memory, the imagery of the poem is lush and occasionally surreal, the narrative sequence may be puzzling, and the syntax often impressionistic. Perhaps it's that the gift of such moments is precisely to disrupt the familiar logic of the quotidian. This makes for an intense and sometimes agrammatical rush of feeling and insight that has no need of translation into the logic of linear thought. That is, the poem, like all the others, resists too much explanation. It resides just as it is in the imagination, which has its own curious way of knowing. And as with Wordsworth, whose phrase Michael borrows, the memorably disruptive spots of time which the collection remembers have the capacity to fructify an entire life.

And then again, the work speaks of stuckness and the loss of vision. Airport lounges invoke a particularly claustrophobic sense of entrapment, a poem about insomnia is a reminder that the capacity for joy involves an intense familiarity with its contrary, and the quest for liberated awareness implies a chafing frustration with the systems that constrain it, internally as well as externally. In the last poem Michael explores this most explicitly. A time comes, he writes, when the beautiful memory of the garden has receded. In fact it's become so distant that you almost give in to the mocking internal voice which says it wasn't real. In the midst of this dark night, even 'that joy which we had once believed to be the tempo of existence' feels like an illusion, and life becomes merely routine, shallow and airless. And then one day, transformation. On an unenthusiastic jaunt to the country with friends, the portal simply opens: 'Light smashed instantly through the walls we had erected around our senses. And we mounted the stairs we knew, although we did not know from where.'

For those of us who knew him, accepting Michael's invitation to follow him into the garden is sure to be painful. The poetry gives us the voice and not the man. Yet somehow the pain is inseparable from joy: that joy which is the tempo of existence. In its fine attention to the spots of time that infuse a life, the writing invokes such vibrant and inextinguishable delight in the living world that in reading it I sense again a trace of the brilliance and freedom we received from our beloved friend when he was alive. This makes the book not just a gift and an invitation, but a teaching. Thank you Linzi and Kobus for sharing this with us.

NOTES ON THE POEMS
by Kobus Moolman

In 2014 Michael sent me an electronic file of his work entitled 'Long poem with 28 short ones'. He had asked for comments. He worked and re-worked this material up until his tragic death in April 2018.

'Spots of Time' (the long poem referred to in the above title) was published in the 2017, June, issue of *New Coin* journal, under the title, 'Cannibal Time', a title which he revised shortly before his death.

'At Lake Sibaya' was published posthumously in *New Contrast* journal, 2018.

'Beach at St Michael's on Sea' and 'Crossberry Flower' were also published posthumously in the American journal, *Five Points*. In the same year.

'Spots of Time' was awarded third prize in the annual DALRO Poetry Award for best poem in *New Coin* journal. But Michael did not get to celebrate this news.

When I decided to publish this collection of Michael's poetry, Linzi Rabinowitz kindly gave me copies of all his poetry on the hard-drive of his laptop. As well as several manilla folders with his print-outs of material.

In consultation with Linzi I have used the most recent versions of all Michael's poems. Interestingly, many of the poems here find their origin in two separate electronic files from 2007: 'Birthday poems' (March) and 'India' (April). These two files contain fragments of seemingly disconnected observations that run in an unbroken fashion, with only a single space between each. In 2009 and then further in 2011 these fragments are divided by a long line drawn underneath to indicate that they are distinct pieces. Each of these pieces are then combined with others, edited and re-edited, until they become their final form here.

Apart from the 28 poems that Michael had originally sent me I included twelve others that I found on his hard-drive Again in consultation with his life partner I have selected only material which in my subjective opinion I have felt to be in a state of completion. There is further material that I have not selected including an album of original digital photos with haiku-like poems, a document on medicinal plants, and several incomplete drafts for poems.

I am grateful to Linzi Rabinowitz for this opportunity to honour Michael's poetry and to help bring it into the light.

Printed in the United States
by Baker & Taylor Publisher Services